To

_____

From

_____

# Little Book

## DEVOTIONS
### 31 DAILY DEVOTIONALS

# Self-Esteem

# Little Book

## DEVOTIONS

# Self-Esteem

Compiled and Edited: Mary Susan Freeman
Cover Design: Kim Russell, Wahoo Designs
Page Layout: Bart Dawson

ISBN 1-58334-270-2

Printed in the United States of America

For All of God's Children

# Table of Contents

A Message to Parents.................................13

1. Jesus and You......................................17
2. You're Wonderful.................................21
3. God Loves You.....................................25
4. Doing What's Right...............................29
5. Don't Be Too Hard on Yourself.............33
6. Loving Everybody
      (Including Yourself)..........................37
7. Good Thinking.....................................41
8. A Loving Family . . . Like Yours!.............45
9. God Wants the Best for You.................49
10. A Rule That's Golden...........................53
11. When You're Sad.................................57
12. You Can't Please Everybody.................61
13. Telling the Truth.................................65
14. Growing Up Every Day.........................69
15. How You Look . . . on the Inside
      and the Outside................................73

16. When People Aren't Nice........................77

17. Being Willing to Try............................81

18. When You Make Mistakes....................85

19. Selfishness Hurts Everybody;
Sharing Helps Everybody..................89

20. It's Wonderful to Be You....................93

21 When You're Worried.............................97

22. Nobody's Perfect................................101

23. Stuff Isn't Us.....................................105

24. Friends Who Behave...........................109

25. Friends Who Are Kind........................113

26. Teamwork Works!...............................117

27. When You Help Other People . . .
You Feel Better about Yourself....121

28. The Person in the Mirror....................125

29. Good Words........................................129

30. Since Jesus Loves You . . . ................133

31. God's Refrigerator..............................137

Bible Verses to Memorize.......................141

# A Message to Parents

Congratulations on picking up this book—it proves that you're vitally interested in the spiritual and intellectual development of your child.

This text is intended to be read by Christian parents to their young children. The book contains 31 brief chapters, one for each day of the month. Each chapter is composed of a Bible verse, a brief story, helpful hints for kids and for parents, and a prayer. Every chapter examines some aspect of a very important topic: self-esteem.

For the next 31 days, try this experiment: read one chapter each night to your child, and then spend a few more moments talking about the chapter's meaning. By the end of the month, you will have had 31 different opportunities to share God's wisdom with your son or daughter, and that's a very good thing.

You know how God's love has transformed your own life. Now it's your turn to share that Good News with the boy or girl whom He has entrusted to your care. Happy reading! And may God continue to bless you and yours, now and forever.

# Self-Esteem

# Jesus and You

# 1

I've loved you the way my Father
has loved me. Make yourselves at home
in my love.

Jesus

John 15:9 MSG

Have you heard the song "Jesus Loves Me"? Probably so. It's a happy song that should remind you of this important fact: Jesus loves you very much.

When you invite Jesus into your heart, He will be your friend forever. If you make mistakes, He'll still be your friend. When you aren't perfect, He'll still love you. If you feel sorry or sad, He can help you feel better.

Yes, Jesus loves you . . . and you should love yourself. So the next time you feel sad about yourself . . . or something that you've done . . . remember that Jesus loves you, your family loves you, and you should feel that way, too.

**There's only one you!** Nobody else in the world is exactly like you. When God made you, He made a very special, one-of-a-kind person. So don't forget this fact: you're very, very, very, very, very special.

## WOW
The dearest friend on earth is only a shadow compared with Jesus Christ.
Oswald Chambers

**Self-esteem starts with you.** Remember this: self-esteem starts at the head of the household and works its way down from there. It's not enough to concern yourself with your child's self-image; you should also strive to become comfortable with your own self-image, too.

Dear Lord,
thank You for Your Son.
Because Jesus loves me,
I will feel good about myself,
my family, and my future.

Amen

# 2

# You're Wonderful

For you made us only a little lower than God, and you crowned us with glory and honor.

● ● ●

Psalm 8:5 NLT

When God made you, He made you in a very special way. In fact, you're a wonderful, one-of-a-kind creation, a special person unlike any other.

Do you realize how special you are? Do you know that God loves you because of who you are (not because of the things you've done)? And do you know that God has important things for you to do? Well, whether you realize it or not, all these things are true.

So the next time you feel bad about something you've done, take a look in the mirror, and remember that you're looking at a wonderfully special person . . . you!

God loves you; your parents love you; your family loves you . . . and that's the way that you should feel about yourself, too.

Accept God's love . . . and love God in return. God loves you for who you are, not because of the things you've done. So open your heart to God's love . . . when you do, you'll feel better about everything, including yourself.

## WOW

Being loved by God, whose opinion matters most, means that we can love ourselves, too.

Gloria Gaither

Remember that God's love doesn't simply flow to your children . . . it flows to you, too. And because God loves you, you can be certain that you, like your child, are wonderfully made and amazingly blessed.

Dear Lord,
I'm certainly not perfect,
but You love me just as I am.
Thank You for Your love and
for Your Son. And, help me to
become the person that
You want me to become.

Amen

# 3 God Loves You

Praise God, everybody! Applaud God,
all people! His love has taken over
our lives; God's faithful ways are eternal.
Hallelujah!

Psalm 117:1-2 MSG

Does God love you? Of course He does! In fact, God loves you so much that He sent His Son Jesus to come to this earth . . . for you! When you accept Jesus into your heart, God gives you a gift that is more precious than gold: that gift is called "eternal life," which means that you will live forever with God in heaven!

You don't have to be perfect to earn God's love . . . you simply have to accept His love by accepting His Son. So do yourself a favor right now: accept God's love with open arms and welcome His Son Jesus into your heart. When you do, your life will be changed today, tomorrow, and forever.

Remember: **God's love for you is too big to understand with your brain** . . . but it's not too big to feel with your heart.

## WOW
If God had a wallet,
your photo would be in it.
Max Lucado

**Express yourself:** Perhaps the most important way that your young child will understand God's love is by experiencing your love. Live your life—and love your child—accordingly.

Dear Lord,
I know that You love me.
I will accept Your love—
and share it—
today and every day.

Amen

# Doing What's
# Right

**4**

The godly walk with integrity;
blessed are their children after them.

❧ ❧ ❧

Proverbs 20:7 NLT

When you know that you're doing what's right, you'll feel better about yourself. Why? Because you have a little voice in your head called your "conscience." Your conscience is a feeling that tells you whether something is right or wrong—and it's a feeling that makes you feel better about yourself when you know you've done the right thing.

Your conscience is an important tool. Pay attention to it!

The more you listen to your conscience, the easier it is to behave yourself. So here's great advice: first, slow down long enough to figure out the right thing to do—and then do it! When you do, you'll be proud of yourself . . . and other people will be proud of you, too.

**When you choose to do the right thing . . . you make everybody happy.** You make your parents happy; you make your teachers happy; you make your friends happy; and you make God happy!

## WOW
Life is a series of choices between
the bad, the good, and the best.
Everything depends on how we choose.
Vance Havner

**Mirror, mirror, on the wall:** When you look into the mirror, you're gazing at the person who is the primary role model for your child. It's a big responsibility, but you—and God—are up to it!

Dear Heavenly Father,
the Bible instructs me to do
what is right. Today, help me
understand what's right . . .
and help me do it.

Amen

# 5

# Don't Be
# Too Hard on
# Yourself

You know the Lord is full of mercy
and is kind.

❦ ❦ ❦

James 5:11 NCV

Face facts: nobody's perfect ... not even you! And remember this: it's perfectly okay not to be perfect. In fact, God doesn't expect you to be perfect, and you shouldn't expect yourself to be perfect, either.

Are you one of those people who can't stand to make a mistake? Do you think that you must please everybody all the time? When you make a mess of things, do you become terribly upset? If so, here's some advice: DON'T BE SO HARD ON YOURSELF!

Even if you're a very good person, you're bound to make mistakes . . . lots of mistakes. When you make a mistake—or when you feel that you haven't "measured up"—you shouldn't become too upset.

Mistakes happen . . . it's simply a fact of life, and it's simply a part of growing up. So don't be too hard on yourself, especially if you've learned something along the way.

**Don't be too hard on yourself**: you don't have to be perfect to be wonderful.

## WOW

The happiest people in the world are not those who have no problems, but the people who have learned to live with those things that are less than perfect.

James Dobson

**Parents aren't perfect**: The perfect parent does not exist. So don't be too hard on yourself when you fall short of absolute perfection (or, for that matter, when you fall short of near-perfection). Do your best, and trust God with the rest.

Dear Lord,
even when I make mistakes,
You love me . . . and even when
I am not perfect, You love me.
And because You love me,
I can feel good about myself,
even when I'm not perfect.

Amen

# 6
# Loving Everybody
## (Including Yourself)

Above all, love each other deeply,
because love covers a multitude of sins.

❦ ❦ ❦

1 Peter 4:8 NIV

The Bible teaches you this lesson: you should love everybody—and the word "everybody" includes yourself. Do you treat yourself with honor and respect? You should. After all, God created you in a very special way, and He loves you very much. And if God thinks you are amazing and wonderful, shouldn't you think about yourself in the same way? Of course you should!

So remember this: God wants you to love everybody, including the person you see when you look in the mirror. And one more thing: when you learn how to respect the person in the mirror, you'll be better at respecting other people, too.

God loves you . . . and you should too.

## WOW
Jesus' stories in Luke 15 tell us that you have never locked eyes with another human being who isn't valuable to God.
Bill Hybels

You know that your child is a unique gift from God . . . make sure that your child hears that message every day . . . from you.

Dear Lord,
today and every day,
I will do my best to love
everybody . . .
including myself.

Amen

# Good Thinking

Those who are pure in their thinking are happy, because they will be with God.

Matthew 5:8 NCV

Do you try to think good thoughts about your friends, your family, and yourself? The Bible says that you should. Do you lift your hopes and your prayers to God many times each day? The Bible says that you should. Do you say "no" to people who want you to do bad things or think bad thoughts? The Bible says that you should.

The Bible teaches you to guard your thoughts against things that are hurtful or wrong. So remember this: When you turn away from bad thoughts and turn instead toward God and His Son Jesus, you will be protected . . . and you will be blessed.

### KiD TiP

**Good thoughts can lead you to some very good places** . . . and bad thoughts can lead elsewhere. So guard your thoughts accordingly.

## WOW

The things we think are the things that feed our souls. If we think on pure and lovely things, we shall grow pure and lovely like them; and the opposite is also true.

Hannah Whitall Smith

### Parent TiP

**Guarding your own thoughts** . . . Most children are incredibly intuitive. Your child may be far more attuned to your thoughts than you realize. So guard your thoughts—and your emotions—accordingly.

Dear Lord,
You teach me that my thoughts
are important to You.
Help me to think good thoughts
and to do good deeds,
today and every day.

Amen

# A Loving Family
## ...Like Yours!

Love must be without hypocrisy.
Detest evil; cling to what is good.
Show family affection to one another with
brotherly love. Outdo one another
in showing honor.

Romans 12:9-10 HCSB

Your family is a wonderful, one-of-a-kind gift from God. And your family members love you very much—what a blessing it is to be loved!

Have you ever really stopped to think about how much you are loved? Your parents love you (of course) and so does everybody else in your family. But it doesn't stop there. You're also an important part of God's family . . . and He loves you more than you can imagine.

What should you do about all the love that comes your way? You should accept it; you should be thankful for it; and you should share it . . . starting now!

**Since you love your family** . . . let them know it by the things you say and the things you do. And, never take your family members for granted; they deserve your very best treatment!

# WOW

There is so much compassion and understanding that is gained when we've experienced God's grace firsthand within our own families.

Lisa Whelchel

**Parental Encouragement 101:** Encouragement is an essential ingredient in healthy parent-child communications. Make sure that you encourage your child by communicating your love, your admiration, and your devotion—and make certain that you do so many times each day.

Dear Lord,
You have given me a family
that cares for me and loves me.
Thank You. I will let my
family know that I love them by
the things that I say and do.
You know that I love my family,
Lord. Now it's my turn
to show them!

Amen

# God Wants
# the Best for You

My purpose is to give life in all its fullness.

John 10:10 HCSB

Here are three things to think about:

1. God loves you.
2. God wants what's best for you.
3. God has a plan for you.

God's plan may not always happen exactly as you want, but remember: God always knows best. Sometimes, even though you may want something very badly, you must still be patient and wait for the right time to get it. And the right time, of course, is determined by God.

Even if you don't get exactly what you want today, you can be sure that God wants what's best for you . . . today, tomorrow, and forever.

**Don't miss out on God's gifts**: Every day is a beautifully wrapped gift from God. Unwrap it, and give thanks to the Giver.

## WOW
Jesus wants Life for us,
Life with a capital L.
John Eldredge

**Parent Tip**

**When Jesus talked about "abundance," was He talking about "money"?** Nope. When Christ talked about abundance, He was concerned with people's spiritual well-being, not their financial well-being. That's a lesson that you must learn . . . and it's a lesson that you must share with your child.

Dear Lord,
You have many, many gifts for
me. I will accept those gifts,
and I will thank You for them . . .
today and forever.

Amen

# 10

# A Rule That's Golden

Don't be selfish . . . Be humble,
thinking of others as better than yourself.

❧ ❧ ❧

Philippians 2:3 NLT

Would you like to make the world a better place and feel better about yourself at the same time? If so, you can start by practicing the Golden Rule.

The Bible teaches us to treat other people with respect, kindness, courtesy, and love. When we do, we make other people happy, we make God happy, and we feel better about ourselves, too.

So if you're wondering how to make the world—and your world—a better place, here's a great place to start: let the Golden Rule be your rule. And if you want to know how to treat other people, ask the person you see every time you look into the mirror. The answer you receive will tell you exactly what to do.

**How would you feel?** When you're trying to decide how to treat another person, ask yourself this question: "How would I feel if somebody treated me that way?" Then, treat the other person the way that you would want to be treated.

## WOW

We hurt other people by being too busy, too busy to notice their needs.

Billy Graham

**Make it your rule, too!** When you become a living, breathing example of the Golden Rule in action, your child will notice, and the results will be better than gold.

Dear Lord,
help me always to do my
very best to treat others as
I wish to be treated.
The Golden Rule is Your rule,
Father; let me also make it mine.

Amen

# 11

# When You're Sad

You will be sad,
but your sadness will become joy.

John 16:20 NCV

Sometimes, you feel happy, and sometimes you don't. When you're feeling sad, here are two very important things you should do:

1. Talk to your parents about your feelings.
2. Talk to God about your feelings.

Talking with your parents is helpful because your mom and dad understand this: The problems that seem VERY BIG to you today probably won't seem so big tomorrow.

Talking with God helps because God hears your prayers and He helps make things better.

So the next time you're sad, don't hold your feelings inside—talk things over with your parents and with God. When you do, you'll feel better . . . and so will they!

## KiD TiP

Everybody feels sad from time to time . . . but the Bible promises in a little while your sadness will turn to joy.

## WOW
God makes the sun shine every day,
even though it is sometimes
hidden behind the clouds.
Corrie ten Boom

## Parent Tip

**In times of hardship:** All families endure times of sadness or hardship; if your troubles seem overwhelming, be willing to seek outside help—starting, of course, with your pastor.

PRAY TIME

Dear Lord,
when I am feeling tired or sad,
I can always talk to You,
and I can always talk to my
parents, too. Thanks for
listening, Lord—and thank You
for parents who are willing to
listen and willing to help.

Amen

# 12

# You Can't Please Everybody

Do you think I am trying to make people accept me? No, God is the One I am trying to please. Am I trying to please people? If I still wanted to please people, I would not be a servant of Christ.

● ● ●

Galatians 1:10 NCV

Are you one of those people who try to please everybody in sight? If so, you'd better watch out! After all, if you worry too much about pleasing your friends, you may not worry enough about pleasing God.

Whom will you try to please today: your God or your pals? The answer to that question should be simple. Your first job is to obey God's rules . . . and that means obeying your parents, too!

So don't worry too much about pleasing your friends or neighbors. Try, instead, to please your Heavenly Father and your parents. No exceptions.

**Please God first.** Then, work very hard to please your parents.

## WOW
Those who follow the crowd
usually get lost in it.
Rick Warren

**Parent Tip**

**Be a good example**: If you are burdened with a "people-pleasing" personality, outgrow it. Realize that you can't please all of the people all of the time (including your children), nor should you attempt to.

Dear Lord,
today I will worry less about
pleasing other people and
more about pleasing You.

Amen

# 13

# Telling the Truth

Tell each other the truth because
we all belong to each other . . . .

❧ ❧ ❧

Ephesians 4:25 ICB

Have you ever said something that wasn't true? And after you said it, were you sorry that you told a lie? Well, if you were sorry, that's not surprising. When you don't tell the truth, you'll usually end up being sorry in the end.

Here's something that you're bound to learn sooner or later, so you might as well learn it right now: Honesty and self-esteem go hand in hand. Why? Because it's hard to feel good about yourself if you're not being honest with other people.

So, if you want to feel better about yourself, do yourself a favor: tell the truth all the time. It's the right thing to do . . . and the best way to live!

**Little white lies? Beware!** You may think that there's a big difference between "little" lies and king-sized ones. Unfortunately, little white lies have a tendency to grow into big trouble . . . in a hurry.

# WOW
God doesn't expect you to be perfect, but he does insist on complete honesty.
Rick Warren

**Honesty at school starts at home**: don't expect teachers to teach the lessons that parents should have already taught!

Dear Lord,
sometimes it's hard to tell
the truth. But even when telling
the truth is difficult, let me
follow Your commandment.
Honesty isn't just the best
policy, Lord; it's Your policy,
and I will obey You by
making it my policy, too.

Amen

# 14

# Growing Up
# Every Day

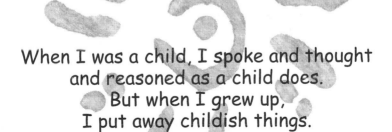

When I was a child, I spoke and thought
and reasoned as a child does.
But when I grew up,
I put away childish things.

🌀 🌀 🌀

1 Corinthians 13:11 NLT

You're growing up day by day, and it's a wonderful thing to watch. Every day, you're learning new things and doing new things. Good for you!

And when should you stop growing up? Hopefully never! That way, you'll always be learning more and doing more.

Do you think it's good to keep growing and growing and growing? If you said "yes," you're right. So remember: you're a very special person today . . . and you'll be just as special when you've grown a little bit more tomorrow.

**Grown-ups still have plenty to learn . . . and so do you!**

# WOW

I'm not what I want to be.
I'm not what I'm going to be.
But, thank God, I'm not what I was!
Gloria Gaither

## Parent Tip

**There's still room to grow**: God is still working in you and through you. Even if you're a mature Christian, you can still grow in the knowledge and love of your Savior every day that you live. And, if you seek to be a righteous example to your children, that's precisely what you should do.

Dear Lord,
thank You for letting me grow
a little bit more every day.
I thank You for the person I am
. . . and for the person
I can become.

Amen

# 15

# How You Look . . . on the Inside and the Outside

Blessed are the pure of heart,
for they will see God.

Matthew 5:8 NIV

Other people see you from the outside, and sometimes people will judge you by the way you look. But God doesn't care how you look on the outside. Why? Because God is wiser than that; God cares about what you are on the inside—God sees your heart.

If you're like most people, you'll worry a little bit about the way you look (or maybe you worry a lot about it). But please don't worry too much about your appearance!

How you look on the outside isn't important . . . but how you feel on the inside is important. So don't worry about trying to impress other people. Instead of trying to impress other kids, try to impress God by being the best person you can be.

**Beauty on the outside isn't important . . .**
beautiful on the inside is.

## WOW

God shows great delight when He sees
people acting in ways that honor Him.

Bill Hybels

**You know that your child is unique and
beautiful . . .** and you must never become
tired of saying so!

Dear Lord,
thank You for watching over me.
Help me be good and to do right.

Amen

# 16

# When People Aren't Nice

You have heard it said,
"Love your neighbor and hate your enemy."
But I tell you: Love your enemies and pray
for those who persecute you, that you may
be sons of your Father in heaven.

❧ ❧ ❧

Matthew 5:43-45 NIV

Sometimes, young people can be very mean. They can make fun of other people, and when they do, it's wrong.

As Christians, we should be kind to everyone. And, if other kids say unkind things to someone, we should never join in.

Today and every day, make sure that you're a person who is known for the kind way that you treat everybody. That's how God wants you to behave.

And if someone says something to you that isn't very nice, don't pay too much attention. Just forgive that person as quickly as you can, and try to move on . . . as quickly as you can.

**Remember to forgive:** If you can't find it in your heart to forgive those who have hurt you, you're hurting yourself more than you're hurting anyone else.

# WOW

When something robs you of your peace of mind, ask yourself if it is worth the energy you are expending on it. If not, then put it out of your mind in an act of discipline. Every time the thought of "it" returns, refuse it.

Kay Arthur

**Don't try to change the other person:** Unless the person you're trying to change is a young child, and unless you are that child's parent or guardian, don't try to change him or her. Why? Because teenagers and adults change when they want to, not when you want them to. (Proverbs 10:14)

Dear Lord,
sometimes it's very hard to
forgive those who have hurt me,
but with Your help, I can
forgive them. Help me to bring
forgiveness into my heart,
so that I can forgive others
just as You have already
forgiven me.

Amen

# 17

# Being Willing to Try

Be on guard. Stand true to what you believe. Be courageous. Be strong.

1 Corinthians 16:13 NLT

When things don't turn out right, it's easy for most of us to give up. But usually, it's wrong. Why are we tempted to give up so quickly? Perhaps it's because we're afraid that we might embarrass ourselves if we tried hard but didn't succeed.

Here's something to remember: if you're having a little trouble getting something done, don't get mad, don't get frustrated, don't get discouraged, and don't give up. Just keep trying . . . and keep believing in yourself.

When you try hard—and keep trying hard—you can do amazing things . . . but if you quit at the first sign of trouble, you'll miss out. So here's a good rule to follow: when you have something that you want to finish, be brave enough (and wise enough) to finish it . . . you'll feel better about yourself when you do.

**If things don't work out at first, don't quit.** If you never try, you'll never know how good you can be.

## WOW

Are you fearful? First, bow your head and pray for God's strength.
Then, raise your head knowing that, together, you and God can handle whatever comes your way.

Jim Gallery

**Perseverance is contagious . . .** and kids usually catch it from their parents.

Dear Lord,
sometimes I feel like giving up.
When I feel that way,
help me do the right thing . . .
and help me finish the work
You want me to do.

Amen

# 18
# When You Make Mistakes

The Lord says, "Forget what happened
before, and do not think about the past.
Look at the new thing I am going to do.
It is already happening. Don't you see it?
I will make a road in the desert
and rivers in the dry land."

Isaiah 43:18-19 NCV

Are you perfect? Certainly not! No matter how hard you try to do the right thing, you're bound to make mistakes every once in a while . . . everybody does.

When you make a mistake, what should you do about it? Here are two things you should do:

1. Try very hard to learn something from your mistake; that way, you won't make that same mistake again.

2. If you have hurt someone—or if you have disobeyed God—you must ask for forgiveness. That means saying you're sorry to the person you hurt . . . and it also means saying you're sorry to God.

So remember this: if you make a mistake, learn from it. And don't repeat it. Because the biggest mistake you can make is to keep making the same mistake over and over and over again.

**Fix it sooner rather than later**: If you make a mistake, the time to make things better is now, not later! The sooner you admit your mistake, the better.

# WOW

God is able to take mistakes,
when they are committed to Him,
and make of them something for our good
and for His glory.

Ruth Bell Graham

**When angels fall . . .** Even your own angelic child may make a mistake on occasion. When the unlikely happens, help your boy or girl understand why the behavior is wrong and how to prevent it in the future.

Dear Lord,
when I make mistakes,
I will admit what I've done,
and I will apologize to the people
I've hurt. You are perfect, Lord;
I am not. I thank You for
Your forgiveness and
for Your love.

Amen

# 19

# Selfishness Hurts Everybody; Sharing Helps Everybody

If you have two shirts, share with the person who does not have one. If you have food, share that too.

❧ ❧ ❧

Luke 3:11 ICB

Learning how to share can be an important way to build better self-esteem. Why? Because when you learn to share your things, you'll know that you've done exactly what God wants you to do—and you'll feel better about yourself.

The Bible teaches that it's better to be generous than selfish. But sometimes, you won't feel like sharing your things, and you'll be tempted to keep everything for yourself. When you're feeling a little bit stingy, remember this: God wants you to share your things with people who need your help.

When you learn to be a more generous person, God will be pleased with you . . . and you'll be pleased with yourself.

**What does the Bible say about sharing?**
It's simple: you should gladly share the
things you have.

## WOW

Nothing is really ours until we share it.
C. S. Lewis

**Parental demonstrations on the art of
sharing**: Your children will learn how to treat
others by watching you (not by listening to
you!). Your acts of kindness and generosity
will speak far louder than words.

Dear Lord,
let me help others in every way
that I can. Jesus served others;
I can, too. Today, I will share
my possessions and my prayers.
And, I will share kind words with
my family and my friends.

Amen

# 20

# It's Wonderful to Be You

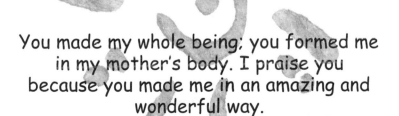

You made my whole being; you formed me
in my mother's body. I praise you
because you made me in an amazing and
wonderful way.

Psalm 139:13-14 NCV

How many people in the world are exactly like you? Only one—the person you see everytime you look in the mirror. In other words, the only person in the world who's exactly like you . . . IS YOU! And that means you're special: special to God, special to your family, special to your friends, and a special addition to God's wonderful world!

But sometimes, when your tired, angry, or sad, you may not feel very special. In fact, you may decide that you're not very special at all . . . but whenever you think like that, you're mistaken.

The Bible says that God made you in "an amazing and wonderful way." So the next time that you start feeling that you don't measure up, remember this: when God made all the people of the earth, He only made one you. And that means you're a V.I.P.

And what is a V.I.P.? A "Very Important Person," of course.

## KiD TiP

**Appearances, appearances, appearances . . .**
Don't be too worried about what you look like
on the outside . . . be more concerned about
the kind of person you are on the inside. God
loves you just as you are . . . and now, it's
your turn to do the same thing.

## WOW

Outside appearances, things like
the clothes you wear or the car you drive,
are important to other people but totally
unimportant to God. Trust God.

Marie T. Freeman

## Parent TiP

**Your kids are watching**: If you're overly
concerned with "keeping up appearances,"
your child will be, too. So, whenever you're
faced with the choice of pleasing your
neighbors or pleasing God, make the right
choice. If you concentrate on pleasing God,
your child will learn what's important . . . and
what's not.

95

Dear Lord,
You know my heart, and You're concerned with the "inner me." Today, I will worry less about what other people think . . . and I'll worry more about what You think.

Amen

# 21

# When You're Worried

Jesus said,
"Don't let your hearts be troubled.
Trust in God, and trust in me."

❧ ❧ ❧

John 14:1 NCV

When you're worried, it helps to talk about the things that are troubling you. And who can you talk to? Well, for starters, you can talk to your parents, and you can talk to God.

If you're worried about something, you can pray about it anytime you want. And remember that God is always listening, and He always wants to hear from you.

So when you're worried, try this plan: talk and pray. Talk to the grown-ups who love you, and pray to the Heavenly Father who made you. The more you talk and the more you pray, the better you'll feel.

## KID TIP

**Worried about something you said or did?**
If you made a mistake yesterday, the day to
fix it is today. Then, you won't have to worry
about it tomorrow.

## WOW

Worry does not empty tomorrow of
its trouble; it empties today of
its strength.

Corrie ten Boom

## Parent Tip

**Controllable worries about uncontrollable
problems:** Carefully divide your areas of
concern into two categories: those you can
control and those you cannot. Resolve never
to waste time or energy worrying about the
latter.

Dear Lord,
when I am worried, I know where
to turn for help: to those who
love me, and to You. Thank You,
for the people who love and care
for me, and thank You, Lord, for
Your love. Because of that love,
I have hope and assurance for
this day and every day.

Amen

# Nobody's Perfect

All have sinned and are not good enough for God's glory.

Romans 3:23 NCV

If you're trying to be perfect, you're trying to do something that's impossible. No matter how much you try, you can't be a perfect person . . . and that's okay.

God doesn't expect you to live a mistake-free life—and neither should you. In the game of life, God expects you to try, but He doesn't always expect you to win. Sometimes, you'll make mistakes, but even then, you shouldn't give up!

So remember this: you don't have to be perfect to be a wonderful person. In fact, you don't even need to be "almost-perfect." You simply must try your best and leave the rest up to God.

**KiD TiP**

**If you hear a little voice inside your head telling you that you're not good enough** . . . don't pay attention to that little voice. God loves you . . . and if you're good enough for God, you're good enough.

## WOW
God is not looking for perfection.
He already saw it in Christ.
He's looking for affection.
Beth Moore

**Parent Tip**

**You know that your kids can't be perfect all the time.** . . . and it's up to you to make sure that they know they're not expected to be perfect all the time.

Dear Lord,
this world has so many
expectations of me, but today
I will not seek to meet
the world's expectations;
I will do my best to meet
Your expectations. I will make
You my ultimate priority, Lord,
by serving You, by praising You,
by loving You, and by
obeying You.

Amen

# 23

# Stuff Isn't Us

Yes, a person is a fool to store up
earthly wealth but not have
a rich relationship with God.

Luke 12:21 NLT

Here's something to remember about stuff: It's not that important!

Lots of people are in love with money and the things that money can buy. God is not. God cares about people, not possessions, and so must you.

You should not be too concerned about the clothes you wear, or the things you own. And above all, don't ever let your self-esteem depend upon the things that you (or your parents) own.

The stuff that you own isn't nearly as important as the love that you feel in your heart—love for your family, love for your friends, and love for your Father in heaven.

**Stuff 101**: The world says, "Buy more stuff." God says, "Stuff isn't important." Believe God.

# WOW

It is not wrong to own things,
but it is wrong for things to own us.

Warren Wiersbe

**Everything we have is on loan from God.** Corrie ten Boom observed, "I have held many things in my hands, and I have lost them all; but whatever I have placed in God's hands, that I still possess." Remember: your real riches are in heaven, so conduct yourself accordingly . . . and teach your children to do likewise.

Dear Lord,
help me value the things in this
world that are really valuable:
my life, my family,
and my relationship with You.

Amen

# 24

# Friends Who Behave

Jacob said, "For what a relief it is
to see your friendly smile.
It is like seeing the smile of God!"

Genesis 33:10 NLT

One way that you can feel better about yourself is by staying out of trouble. And one way that you can stay out of trouble is by making friends with people who, like you, want to do what's right.

Are your friends the kind of kids who encourage you to behave yourself? If so, you've chosen your friends wisely. But if your friends try to get you in trouble, perhaps it's time to think long and hard about making some new friends.

Whether you know it or not, you're probably going to behave like your friends behave. So pick out friends who make you want to behave better, not worse. When you do, you'll feel better about yourself . . . a whole lot better.

## KiD TiP

If you choose friends who behave them-selves . . . you'll be far more likely to behave yourself, too.

## WOW

Do you want to be wise?
Choose wise friends.
Charles Swindoll

## Parent Tip

Do you want your child to choose well-behaved friends! If so, talk openly to your child about the wisdom of choosing friends who behave themselves.

Dear Lord,
other people may want me
to misbehave, but You want me
to behave myself. And that's
what I want, too—I want to do
what's right. So help me do
the right thing, Lord,
even when it's hard.

Amen

# 25
## Friends Who Are Kind

A friend loves you all the time.
❦ ❦ ❦
Proverbs 17:17 ICB

*A*re your friends kind to you? And are your friends nice to other people, too? If so, congratulations! If not, it's probably time to start looking for a few new friends. After all, it's really not very much fun to be around people who aren't nice to everybody.

The Bible teaches that a pure heart is a wonderful blessing. It's up to each of us to fill our hearts with love for God, love for Jesus, and love for all people. When we do, we feel better about ourselves.

Do you want to be the best person you can be? Then invite the love of Christ into your heart and share His love with your family and friends. And remember that lasting love always comes from a pure heart . . . like yours!

**Remember the first rule of friendship:** it's the Golden one, and it starts like this: "Do unto others . . ." You should practice the Golden Rule, and your friends should practice it, too.

# WOW
For better or worse, you will eventually become more and more like your friends. So why not choose friends who make you better, not worse?

Marie T. Freeman

### Parent Tip

**Help from the sidelines:** As parents, we can't make friendships for our children, but we can coach them on the art of making friends. All of us, whether youngsters or grown-ups, make friends by treating others as we wish to be treated. And if that sounds suspiciously like the Golden Rule, that's because it is the Golden Rule.

Dear Lord,
I thank You for friends who help
me feel better about myself.
Help me to choose my friends
wisely, and help me treat
my friends like I want
them to treat me.

Amen

# 26

# Teamwork Works!

A kingdom that is divided cannot continue,
and a family that is divided
cannot continue.

Mark 3:24-25 NCV

Helping other people can be fun! When you help others, you feel better about yourself—and you'll know that God approves of what you're doing.

When you learn how to cooperate with your family and friends, you'll soon discover that it's more fun when everybody works together.

So do everybody a favor: learn better ways to share and better ways to cooperate. It's the right thing to do.

**Cooperation pays**: When you cooperate with your friends and family, you'll feel good about yourself—and your family and friends will feel good about you, too.

# WOW
One person working alone doesn't accomplish much. Success is the result of people pulling together.
John Maxwell

## Parent Tip

**Teaching cooperation**: You know that your children can accomplish much more in life by working cooperatively with others. So it's up to you to teach the fine art of cooperation. And make no mistake: the best way to teach the art of cooperation is by example.

Dear Lord,
help me learn to be kind,
courteous, and cooperative with
my family and with my friends.

Amen

# 27

# When You Help Other People . . . You Feel Better about Yourself

So let us try to do what makes peace and helps one another.

Romans 14:19 NCV

Sometimes we would like to help make the world a better place, but we're not sure how to do it. Jesus told the story of the "Good Samaritan," a man who helped a fellow traveler when no one else would. We, too, should be good Samaritans when we find people who need our help. A good place to start helping other people is at home. And, of course, we should also offer our help at school and at church.

Another way that we can help other people is to pray for them. God always hears our prayers, so we should talk with Him as often as we can. When we do, we're not only doing a wonderful thing for the people we pray for, but we're also doing a wonderful thing for ourselves, too. Why? Because we feel better about ourselves when we're helping other people. And the more we help others, the better we should feel about ourselves.

**Someone very near you may need a helping hand or a kind word,** so keep your eyes open, and look for people who need your help, whether at home, at church, or at school.

# WOW

Do all the good you can. By all the means you can. In all the ways you can. In all the places you can. At all the times you can. To all the people you can. As long as you can.

John Wesley

## Parent Tip

**Preach, teach, and reach . . . out!** When it comes to teaching our children about helping others, our sermons are not as important as our service. Charity should start at home—with parents—and work its way down the family tree from there.

Dear Lord,
let me help others in every way
that I can. Jesus served others;
I can, too. I will serve other
people with my good deeds
and with my prayers,
today and every day.

Amen

# 28

# The Person in the Mirror

Unfailing love surrounds those
who trust the LORD.

Psalm 32:10 NLT

Do you really like the person you see when you look in the mirror? You should! After all, the person in the mirror is a very special person who is made—and loved—by God,

In fact, you are loved in many, many ways: God loves you, your parents love you, and your family loves you, for starters. So you should love yourself, too.

So here's something to think about: since God thinks you're special, and since so many people think you're special, isn't it about time for you to agree with them? Of course it is! It's time to say, "You're very wonderful and very special," to the person you see in the mirror.

**Remember: God loves you, and lots of people love you, too** . . . so it's only proper that you should admit that you're a very special person.

# WOW

A healthy self-identity is seeing yourself as God sees you—no more and no less.

Josh McDowell

**Parents have mirrors, too.** If you want your child to admire the person he or she sees in the mirror, then you should admire the person you see in the mirror.

Dear Lord,
I have so much to learn and so
many ways to improve myself,
but You love me just as I am.
Thank You for Your love and
for Your Son. And, help me to
become the person that
You want me to become.

Amen

# 29

# Good Words

Watch the way you talk. Let nothing
foul or dirty come out of your mouth.
Say only what helps, each word a gift.

Ephesians 4:29 MSG

Your words can help people . . . or not. Make certain that you're the kind of person who says helpful things, not hurtful things. You'll feel better about yourself when you help other people feel better about themselves.

Do you like for people to say kind words to you? Of course you do! And that's exactly how other people feel, too. That's why it's so important to say things that make people feel better, not worse.

Everybody needs to hear kind words, and that's exactly the kind of words they should hear from you!

**KiD TiP**

**When you're talking to somebody, ask yourself this question:** "How can I be helpful?"

# WOW
When you talk, choose the very
same words that you would use if
Jesus were looking over your shoulder.
Because He is.
Marie T. Freeman

**Parent Tip**

**It's up to you:** Make certain that your little abode is a haven of encouragement for every member of your family. You do so by checking your gripes and disappointments at the front door . . . and encouraging everybody else to do likewise!

Dear Lord,
You hear every word that I say.
Help me remember to speak
words that are honest,
kind, and helpful.

Amen

# 30

# Since Jesus Loves You . . .

And I am convinced that nothing
can ever separate us from his love.
Whether we are high above the sky or
in the deepest ocean, nothing in all
creation will ever be able to separate us
from the love of God that is revealed
in Christ Jesus our Lord.

❁ ❁ ❁

Romans 8:38–39 NLT

Do you know that Jesus loves you? And have you thought about exactly what His love should mean to you? Well, Christ's love should make you feel better about your life, your family, your future, and yourself.

There's an old song that says, "What a friend we have in Jesus." Those words are certainly true! When you invite Him into your heart, Jesus will be your friend forever.

Jesus wants you to have a happy, healthy life. He wants you to behave yourself, and He wants you to feel good about yourself. And now, it's up to you to do your best to live up to the hopes and dreams of your very best friend: Jesus.

**Jesus loves you** . . . His love is amazing, it's wonderful, and it's meant for you.

## WOW
I am truly happy with Jesus Christ.
I couldn't live without Him.
Ruth Bell Graham

**Parent Tip**

**Be imaginative:** There are so many ways to say "I love you." Find them. Put love notes in lunch pails and on pillows; hug relentlessly; laugh, play, and pray with abandon. Remember that love is highly contagious, and that your task, as a parent, is to ensure that your child catches it from you.

Dear Lord,
Your love is so wonderful that
I can't really imagine it,
but I can share it . . .
and I will . . .
today and every day.

Amen

# 31
## God's Refrigerator

We know how much God loves us,
and we have put our trust in him.
God is love, and all who live in love
live in God, and God lives in them.

❧ ❧ ❧

1 John 4:16 NLT

If God had a refrigerator in heaven, your picture would be on it! And that fact should make you feel very good about the person you are and the person you can become.

God's love for you is bigger and more wonderful than you can imagine. So do this, and do it right now: accept God's love with open arms and welcome His Son Jesus into your heart. When you do, you'll feel better about yourself . . . and your life will be changed forever.

**What a friend you have in Jesus:** Jesus loves you, and He offers you eternal life with Him in heaven. Welcome Him into your heart. Now!

## WOW
Jesus: the proof of God's love.
Philip Yancey

**You know that "God is love."** Now, it's your responsibility to make certain that your children know it, too.

Dear Lord,
thank You for Your love.
Your love is amazing and
wonderful. Because You love me,
Father, I can feel good about
myself, my world, and my
eternal life with You in heaven.

Amen

# Bible Verses
# to Memorize

Tell each other the truth
because we all belong
to each other . . . .

❀ ❀ ❀

Ephesians 4:25 ICB

Here is my final advice:
Honor God and
obey his commands.

Ecclesiastes 12:13 ICB

143

Without wavering,
let us hold tightly to
the hope we say we have,
for God can be trusted to
keep his promise.

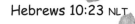

Hebrews 10:23 NLT

I wait quietly before God,
for my hope is in him.

Psalm 62:5 NLT

Always be humble and
gentle. Be patient and
accept each other with love.

Ephesians 4:2 ICB

A wise person pays attention
to correction that will
improve his life.

Proverbs 15:31 ICB

Jesus Christ is the same
yesterday, today, and forever.

Hebrews 13:8 HCSB

# I am the vine;
# you are the branches . . .
# apart from me you can
# do nothing.

John 15:5 NIV

Rejoice in the Lord always.
I will say it again:
Rejoice!

Philippians 4:4 HCSB

# Show respect for all people. Love the brothers and sisters of God's family.

❧ ❧ ❧

1 Peter 2:17 ICB

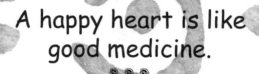

A happy heart is like
good medicine.

Proverbs 17:22 NCV

Remember what you are taught.
And listen carefully to
words of knowledge.

❋ ❋ ❋

Proverbs 23:12 ICB

Jesus answered,
"If anyone loves Me,
he will keep My word."

John 14:23 HCSB

So these three things continue forever: faith, hope, and love. And the greatest of these is love.

🕮 🕮 🕮

1 Corinthians 13:13 ɪᴄʙ

For to me to live is Christ,
and to die is gain.

Philippians 1:21 KJV

Create in me a pure heart,
O God, and renew
a steadfast spirit within me.

Psalm 51:10 NIV

**Little Book Devotions** help parents and children discuss important Biblical themes by relating those themes to the challenges of everyday life. These books are intended to be read *by* parents *to* children. Current titles include:

**Little Book Devotions** Honesty
**Little Book Devotions** Kindness
**Little Book Devotions** Patience
**Little Book Devotions** Forgiveness
**Little Book Devotions** Self-Control
**Little Book Devotions** Sharing
**Little Book Devotions** Attitude
**Little Book Devotions** Obedience

Additional titles are coming soon.

Little Book Devotions are available in LifeWay Christian Stores.